*S*PORTS *GREAT*

KEITH
VAN HORN

BASKETBALL

SPORTS GREAT CHARLES BARKLEY
REVISED EDITION
0-7660-1004-X/ Macnow

SPORTS GREAT LARRY BIRD
0-89490-368-3/ Kavanagh

SPORTS GREAT MUGGSY BOGUES
0-89490-876-6/ Rekela

SPORTS GREAT KOBE BRYANT
0-7660-1264-6/ Macnow

SPORTS GREAT PATRICK EWING
0-89490-369-1/ Kavanagh

SPORTS GREAT KEVIN GARNETT
0-7660-1263-8/ Macnow

SPORTS GREAT ANFERNEE HARDAWAY
0-89490-758-1/ Rekela

SPORTS GREAT GRANT HILL
0-7660-1467-3/ Hill

SPORTS GREAT JUWAN HOWARD
0-7660-1065-1/ Savage

SPORTS GREAT MAGIC JOHNSON
REVISED AND EXPANDED
0-89490-348-9/ Haskins

SPORTS GREAT MICHAEL JORDAN
REVISED EDITION
0-89490-978-9/ Aaseng

SPORTS GREAT JASON KIDD
0-7660-1001-5/ Torres

SPORTS GREAT KARL MALONE
0-89490-599-6/ Savage

SPORTS GREAT STEPHON MARBURY
0-7660-1265-4/ Savage

SPORTS GREAT REGGIE MILLER
0-89490-874-X/ Thornley

SPORTS GREAT ALONZO MOURNING
0-89490-875-8/ Fortunato

SPORTS GREAT DIKEMBE MUTOMBO
0-7660-1267-0/ Torres

SPORTS GREAT HAKEEM OLAJUWON
REVISED EDITION
0-7660-1268-9/ Knapp

SPORTS GREAT SHAQUILLE O'NEAL
REVISED EDITION
0-7660-1003-1/ Sullivan

SPORTS GREAT SCOTTIE PIPPEN
0-89490-755-7/ Bjarkman

SPORTS GREAT MITCH RICHMOND
0-7660-1070-8/ Grody

SPORTS GREAT DAVID ROBINSON
REVISED EDITION
0-7660-1077-5/ Aaseng

SPORTS GREAT DENNIS RODMAN
0-89490-759-X/ Thornley

SPORTS GREAT JOHN STOCKTON
0-89490-598-8/ Aaseng

SPORTS GREAT ISIAH THOMAS
0-89490-374-8/ Knapp

SPORTS GREAT CHRIS WEBBER
0-7660-1069-4/ Macnow

SPORTS GREAT DOMINIQUE WILKINS
0-89490-754-9/ Bjarkman

For Other *Sports Great Titles* call:
(800) 398-2504

SPORTS GREAT

KEITH
VAN HORN

Carl W. Grody

—SPORTS GREAT BOOKS—

Enslow Publishers, Inc.

40 Industrial Road   PO Box 38
Box 398   Aldershot
Berkeley Heights, NJ 07922 Hants GU12 6BP
USA   UK

http://www.enslow.com

*To McKenna, who hopes to someday
illustrate Daddy's books.*

Library of Congress Cataloging-in-Publication Data

Grody, Carl W.
    Sports great Keith Van Horn / Carl W. Grody
        p. cm. — (Sports great books)
        Includes index.
        ISBN 0-7660-1471-1 $17.95
        1. Van Horn, Keith, 1975—Juvenile literature. 2. Basketball players—
United States—Biography—Juvenile literature. [1. Van Horn, Keith, 1975–
2. Basketball players.] I. Title: Keith Van Horn. II. Title. III. Series.
GV884.V365 G76   2001
796.323'092—dc21

                                                                00-010865

Printed in the United States of America

10 9 8 7 6 5 4 3 2 1

To Our Readers: We have done our best to make sure all Internet addresses in this book
were active and appropriate when we went to press. However, the author and
the publisher have no control over and assume no liability for the material available
on those Internet sites or on other Web sites they may link to. Any comments or
suggestions can be sent by e-mail to comments@enslow.com or to the address on the
back cover.

Illustration Credits: Fernando Medina/NBA Photos, p. 49; Nathaniel S.
Butler/NBA Photos, p. 46; NBA Photos, p. 60; Noren Trotman/NBA Photos,
p. 57; University of Utah, pp. 8, 10, 14, 16, 19, 21, 24, 28, 30, 34, 36, 40, 43;
Vincent Manniello/NBA Photos, p. 54.

Cover Illustration: Nathaniel S. Butler/NBA Photos.

Contents

Acknowledgments

The author would like to thank the following for their cooperation with this book: the University of Utah's Sports Information Director for Men's Basketball, Mike Lageschulte, and his staff; the University of Memphis sports information office; and Memphis head basketball coach John Calipari.

Chapter 1

Pressure

Keith Van Horn did not want to be there.

There were just three-tenths of a second left in the game. Van Horn's team, the University of Utah, trailed Southern Methodist by a point. Utah had already won the regular season championship of the Western Athletic Conference (WAC), and the Utes—especially Head Coach Rick Majerus—thought having to win the WAC's postseason tournament as well was too much to ask. As Van Horn said, "A 15–1 record speaks for itself."

But now that the game was on the line, Van Horn was ready. He was Utah's all-time leading scorer. He would later become the WAC's all-time leading scorer, too. And everybody in the Thomas & Mack Arena in Las Vegas knew Van Horn would get the ball.

Teammate Andre Miller lobbed the ball toward Van Horn near the foul line. Van Horn caught the ball behind his head. He was off-balance, and a defender was in his face. He launched the shot. It hit nothing but net. The Utes celebrated wildly as the scoreboard flashed the final score: Utah 59, SMU 58.

"I overran the ball a little bit," Van Horn said, "but credit Andre. He made a great pass."

SMU was stunned but not surprised. "All-American

Keith Van Horn flies through the air with grace, skill, and precision. By the end of his senior year at the University of Utah, Van Horn had been named the WAC's Player of the Year three years in a row.

players make All-American plays," said SMU Head Coach Mike Dement.

Dement was disappointed, but he knew Utah was dangerous—especially the six-foot ten-inch, 240-pound forward from Diamond Bar, California. This was the same man who had been the WAC's Player of the Year for the past three years.

"Nobody has been able to stop him," Dement said. "That's mainly because he can do anything he wants to. He can post up on you and become an imposing presence inside, or he can move outside and hit the three. It's impossible to control him."

It was also impossible for Van Horn to enjoy the win. Utah had to play again the next night in the semifinals against the University of New Mexico.

Van Horn must have had a feeling of déjà vu during the game against the Lobos. He struggled for most of the game, scoring just 8 points, but the game was tied with seconds left. There was a battle for a loose ball, and Van Horn snagged it. Without thinking, he turned and fired. For the second night in a row, he tickled twine as the buzzer sounded. Utah won again on a heroic shot by its senior co-captain.

The Utes mobbed Van Horn. Majerus jumped in the air and pumped his fist. But again, the celebration was short. Utah had to play again, the very next night, for the WAC Tournament championship.

It was not surprising that the Utes did not like the WAC Tournament.

"If you polled 15 of [the] 16 coaches [in the WAC], exempting myself, I would say that they would acknowledge that we are the WAC champs," Majerus said before the tournament even started.

The main reason for that was Van Horn. He could have gone to the NBA the previous year, but he resisted the

After nailing the game-wining shot at the WAC Tournament, Van Horn ran wildly up and down the court. He had just moved one step closer to his dream of playing in the Final Four.

temptation. He was getting married, and he wanted his wife and daughter to adjust to family life before he turned pro. He also had promised his late father that he would graduate from college. And he had made a promise to himself on the court—to lead Utah to its first Final Four since 1966.

Keith Van Horn was determined to keep all his promises.

Chapter 2

High School Star

Keith Van Horn was born October 23, 1975, in Fullerton, California. There was never any doubt that he would be big. His father, Ken, was six feet eight inches. His mother, May, was six feet one inch.

Keith was blessed with more than just size. He also had a passion for basketball. He started playing when he was five years old in his hometown of Diamond Bar, California. He was eight when he first said he would play in the NBA. He played in every pickup game he could find. When he got older, he traveled to nearby Los Angeles to play against tougher competition.

"I just played as much as I could," Van Horn said. "I didn't have a routine. I just went out and played."

Keith's walls were covered with posters of Michael Jordan and Magic Johnson. He was a fan of the Los Angeles Lakers, who played their games less than an hour from his house.

His family life was stable. "My parents encouraged me without forcing anything," Van Horn said. "I can remember only three games in my career that my mom missed.

My dad taught me all the lessons I needed to be successful in life."

Ken Van Horn owned a fire-sprinkler business. His size may have been intimidating, but his attitude was not. He was very thoughtful. He was famous in the family for sitting in his chair, thinking, while others argued.

"My dad taught me so much about discipline, kindness, and the need to back up your commitments," Keith said. "When you start something, you finish it. . . . I have my father's mannerisms and easygoing nature. I guess my entire approach to life is exactly like my father. I'm a duplicate of him."

"I see a lot of his father in him," Majerus agreed. "He doesn't 'big-time' anybody or anything. He has an air of authenticity about him that is very, very refreshing."

The authenticity appeared in his game, too. Keith first dunked when he was twelve years old. At the time, he stood five feet eleven inches. He also played a lot of basketball in his backyard against his siblings, brother Jeff and sister Kim.

"I remember the first time he beat me in a one-on-one game," Jeff said. "He came into the house yelling, he was so excited. He did the same thing when he beat our sister."

Kim was also a great athlete. She played volleyball for the University of Southern California. Keith was fourteen when he first beat Kim in hoops; she was twenty-three. It may have been a sign that Keith was maturing into the great player he always wanted to be.

Keith became a serious prospect as a junior at Diamond Bar High School. That season, he averaged 22 points and 9 rebounds a game. But he really caught the eyes of college recruiters during the summer leagues between his junior and senior years. One of those was Utah Assistant Coach Donny Daniels. The Utes were looking

When he was young, Keith loved to play one-on-one with his father. Keith's very first slam dunk was at the age of twelve.

for a replacement for star forward Josh Grant, and they found him in Keith.

"[Keith] was the same guy—same size, same kind of skills," Daniels said. "The only thing he doesn't do as well as Josh is pass. When I saw him play, he had 29 points, 12 boards, 8 assists, and knocked down 4 threes. I said, 'This is the guy.'"

Majerus was convinced when he saw Keith's work ethic. He watched Keith play two games one summer morning in Santa Barbara. Then Keith hopped in the car with his mom and headed to Pomona to play in another league that night.

"That drive is a nerve-wracking, bumper-to-bumper, 150-mile drive," Majerus said. "Most kids would be pool-side by the afternoon, but Keith showed me how much he loved to play. He got there early and stayed late. . . . I grabbed a sandwich and drove straight there. It was a three-hour drive. When I saw Keith walk in that gym with his mom, I knew this was a kid who loved to play the game. I knew he was a kid I'd like to coach."

Keith decided quickly that he wanted to play for Majerus, too. Keith made his only recruiting visit to Utah. Before the weekend was over, he decided to go to Utah.

Keith made the announcement in November of his senior season at Diamond Bar. "I'm happy to get it over with early," Keith said. "Utah really has everything I want. I want to be a physical therapy major, and they've got a good medical center. And Coach Majerus is a coach I can trust. He knows a lot about the game, and he's well respected."

With that decision made, Keith was free to enjoy his senior season. He averaged 29 points per game and led the Brahmas to the league championship game against Ayala High School.

After being a high school star, Keith knew he wanted to continue basketball in college. It took only one trip to the University of Utah for him to decide to play for the Utes.

Ayala and Diamond Bar were the top two teams in the league, and the game was close all the way. With six seconds left and Diamond Bar down by one, Keith blocked a shot, grabbed the ball, and hurried downcourt. He was fouled with two-tenths of a second left.

With the league championship literally on the line, Keith made two free throws for the win. He later called it one of the greatest games he ever played in.

Chapter 3

Adjustment Period

It was hard to tell which was a bigger adjustment for Van Horn: college life in Utah or playing for Rick Majerus.

Utah was like another planet compared to California. The nearby Wasatch Mountains dominated the landscape, and there were fewer people than in the greater Los Angeles area where Van Horn grew up. Majerus joked, "Fifty percent of the people who live out here are in the federal witness protection program."

"People are very nice here," Van Horn said. "It's not the kind of place where people come running up to you to talk about a game. I like being left alone."

If that was true, Majerus was the wrong coach for him. Majerus was the son of a steelworker in Sheboygan, Wisconsin. Cut from his high school basketball team, Majerus graduated from Marquette University in 1970 and became an assistant for Marquette Head Coach Al McGuire. He was still with Marquette when the Warriors won the 1977 NCAA national championship. He was later the head coach for Marquette, and then Ball State University. He became the head coach at Utah in 1989.

Majerus lived a quirky private life. He moved into a hotel when he reached town and never bothered to move

Playing for Rick Majerus was harder than Keith Van Horn had expected. Majerus believed that the best way to make his players better was to push them.

out. He was divorced, with no kids, so his players became his children. Like old-fashioned fathers, Majerus decided the best way to make his players into better people was to push them—hard.

He pushed Van Horn hardest of all. He rarely said good things about Van Horn in the newspapers. He complained about Van Horn's bad defense or his freshman mistakes. After one game, he tore a statistics sheet out of Van Horn's hands and yelled, "These stats mean nothing!" He even made him cry during a film session.

After that episode, Majerus met Van Horn in a bagel shop to to have a talk with him. "I told him, 'Keith, I'm only so hard on you because I know how good you can be,'" Majerus said. "I'm harder on guys with talent because I feel an obligation to bring that out." Richie Smith, a long-time friend of Majerus, explained the coach's approach:

> Rick was criticized some for his treatment of Keith. He never gave Keith a lot of public applause, and that bothered some people. But he saw what the finished product could be. . . . He's a demanding coach. In the beginning, it's a huge adjustment for kids coming into the program. But he's also been here long enough now that both players and their parents have seen it work. They have seen the transformation of Rick's kids—on and off the court. They see what happens when a kid spends four or five years with Rick.

Van Horn's personal life transformed, too, starting with the second day of school. He went to a campus bonfire and met a local girl, Amy Sida of nearby Sandy, Utah. Amy was a freshman, too, majoring in nursing. The two quickly became a couple.

On the court, the pressure was on Van Horn. He was replacing Josh Grant, who was the WAC Player of the Year twice. Utah also lost three other starters from the

Jumping through the air to block baskets was never a problem for Keith. But when he entered Utah at six feet nine inches and 190 pounds, he was easy to push around on the court. Van Horn worked very hard to increase both his skills and strength.

previous year's team. That group went 24–7, won the WAC regular-season championship and won a game in the NCAA Tournament. The new Utes were young. Eight of them were either freshmen or sophomores.

Van Horn was no longer the tallest player on the court, either. In high school, he dominated because he was six feet nine inches. But in college, his thin frame for someone that tall—just 190 pounds—made him easy to push around.

Van Horn had 15 points and 17 rebounds in his first college game, a 105–64 rout of the University of Southern California. Three nights later, Van Horn popped in 27 points and added 10 rebounds in a win against Cal State–Irvine. But after that game, Majerus grumbled, "He was in the right spot at the right time. He's going to be a good player, but he's far from there."

Majerus was right. In early December, Weber State blew out Utah, and Majerus yanked Van Horn from the game for "instruction." Less than a week later, Van Horn was overwhelmed by fourteenth-ranked Arizona in an 88–81 loss. He scored 24 but could not stop Arizona's big men.

"The key difference was youth," Majerus said. "We've got young players, not mature bodies and not a lot of bodies. They got those boards inside on Van Horn. He just isn't tough enough yet or strong enough."

Van Horn played one of his best games when Utah traveled to Cal State–Fullerton, just a few miles from his hometown. Playing in front of friends and relatives, he scored 20 points and grabbed 8 rebounds in a three-point win.

But the win must have been bittersweet. Van Horn's dad was sick. He needed a heart transplant. Without it, he would not live for long.

Chapter 4

Hard Times

Majerus got the call early in the morning of January 26, 1994. It was May Van Horn. Ken Van Horn had died of a heart attack. She wanted Majerus to tell Keith.

She picked the right person to deliver the news. Majerus knew all about heart disease and death. He'd missed most of the 1989–90 season because of a bad heart; he had seven bypasses. Majerus had also lost his own father, so he knew what Van Horn would go through.

"We went out at two thirty in the morning to a coffee shop," Van Horn said. "We just talked about things, our fathers, other things like that. He helped me through a very hard time in my life. He kind of gave me a cheat sheet of the kind of feelings I was going to have and what I was going to go through."

"He was just overcome with the sadness of it, and he was overcome with grief and the finality of it," Majerus said. "I think Keith had the concern we all have. Why does that happen? Where do you go? Will you ever see anyone again? I think he feels the same thing I do [about my dad]. . . . He feels cheated and he feels a sense of longing and a sense of loneliness. That continuum of life is not there."

When the sun rose, Van Horn caught a plane to California. Majerus told him to take his time getting back.

Despite the off-the-court hardships Van Horn endured his first year at Utah, including the death of his father, he played outstanding basketball. He received the WAC's Freshman of the Year award.

"I told him I don't care about basketball," Majerus said. "I don't care if he plays next week or doesn't play next week. . . . Keith is devastated. I lost my dad, and it was the hardest thing I've had to deal with in my own life."

On the court, the Utes were falling apart. One player, Darroll Wright, quit the team twice in three weeks. Phil Dixon, the Utes' only senior starter, had a knee operation and missed the rest of the season. Van Horn missed three games and more than a week of classes.

Van Horn returned in early February for a game at Wyoming. He made just two of nine shots and scored 9 points. He also played more minutes than he expected because the team was short of players. To make things worse, three Utes were injured in the second half. Utah lost for the fifth time in six games. Afterward, Van Horn barely made it through the tunnel before breaking down.

"Everything—my dad's death, our losing, the team dissension—finally overcame me," Van Horn said. " I wondered if I should even have come back this season. I almost broke down right on the court."

Utah ended the season by getting crushed, 96–65, in the first round of the WAC Tournament by Brigham Young. Utah finished 14–14. That was Majerus's worst record with the Utes.

Despite the turmoil, Van Horn was named the WAC's Freshman of the Year and a member of the All-WAC team. He averaged 18.4 points and 8.5 rebounds.

"I came in my first year expecting to help out where I could," Van Horn said. "We had some experienced players, and I thought we'd win the WAC title, but then everything started swirling around. I didn't think I'd have the kind of impact I had. I just tried to fight through everything."

"I don't know how he made it through that," Majerus admitted. "An eighteen-year-old kid away from home. He went through a lot."

Chapter 5

Sophomore Season

Van Horn did not rest on his laurels during the summer. He played in the U.S. Olympic Festival in July. He also worked out hard. His normal day included pick-up basketball games, an hour on the exercise bike, and four hours of weight lifting.

But not everything was rosy. In August, his girlfriend, Amy Sida, told him she was pregnant. He proposed to her, and she accepted. But she got upset when he would not set a date for the wedding. When she realized he was marrying her out of a sense of obligation, she broke up with him.

"Oftentimes, it's not the best idea to get married just because you have a child," Van Horn said. "Had we gotten married right away, I think we would have had a lot of problems."

Amy Sida dropped out of school and moved in with her parents. Her own self-esteem was at an all-time low. Meanwhile, Van Horn was still in school, still playing major college basketball and still on track to achieve his dream. "There was a little resentment towards the big guy," Sida admitted.

But Van Horn helped her through the tough times. He told her to believe in herself. He told her that she could be anything that she wanted to be.

On the court, Utah opened the season against Indiana University in the Maui Classic in Hawaii. Van Horn got in foul trouble and scored only 2 points in the first half, but the Utes won, 77–72.

The next night, Utah lost to seventh-ranked Maryland. The next day, they lost to thirteenth-ranked Michigan. Van Horn made the all-tournament team, but Majerus was livid about a behind-the-back dribble Van Horn tried on a fast break against Michigan. He was also unhappy about the way Maryland manhandled Van Horn under the boards.

"Keith and I are going to have a big meeting on Friday about what this game is all about," Majerus stewed.

Things were not going well at home, either. While Van Horn was in Hawaii, Amy Sida told her parents that she was pregnant. Her father was especially mad. He thought Van Horn made her tell them by herself. But Amy had made the decision on her own. Van Horn did not know what was going on.

"Dad thought Keith was scared to tell him," Amy said. "I really feared for Keith. It's scary when you tell your dad something like this. . . . They totally embraced us. It took only about a month."

May Van Horn embraced the idea of an immediate marriage, but Amy's parents—after recovering from the initial shock—told the couple to take their time. Van Horn and Amy held firm in their decision not to get married, a choice that was supported by Amy's preacher.

Free to concentrate on basketball, Van Horn started playing well with the Utes. They won their next eight games by an average of 26 points. When the WAC regular season started in January, Utah was 9–2.

But in the first WAC game, Van Horn was passive

The skill that Van Horn demonstrated on the court surprised everyone. Still, both Van Horn and his coach knew that he needed to work on his defensive skills if he wanted to play in the NBA.

against BYU, and the Cougars slapped the Utes, 64–57. Van Horn scored only 15 points and the Utes shot just 42 percent against BYU's zone defense.

Van Horn learned from that loss. He scored 26 in his next game, an eight-point win at Fresno State. He scored a career-high 28 points with 11 rebounds against the Air Force Academy. He had 24 points, 13 rebounds, and 4 blocks in a win over Hawaii.

"I was watching film after the BYU game, and I came to the realization of what I could be doing, what I should be doing and what I wasn't doing," Van Horn said. "After the BYU game, I was disgusted with myself. There's no excuse for playing like that."

Even Majerus noticed a difference. "This was maybe his best defensive game as a Ute," Majerus said after the Hawaii game.

Van Horn was named the WAC Player of the Week at the end of January. In February, he scored 37 in a win over Wyoming, and Utah clinched a tie for the WAC regular-season title by beating Fresno State by 30 points. In that game, Van Horn had 22 points and 6 rebounds.

"This guy is just wasting his time in college," said Fresno State Head Coach Gary Colson. "My gosh, he's big-time."

Van Horn, now a business major, also felt the presence of his father. "My dad always wanted to see me get a college degree and play in the NBA," he said. "Sometimes when I feel lazy and don't want to work hard in practice, that's when I hear him. And it motivates me."

Utah won the WAC championship by beating BYU in the last game of the regular season, 87–79. Van Horn scored only 10 points, but four other Utes scored in double figures as well. It was Van Horn's first win over BYU, and he later called it one of his most memorable games.

Van Horn was named the WAC's Player of the Year, and Utah went into the WAC Tournament in New Mexico ranked No. 21 in the country. The Utes struggled to beat San Diego State in the first round. But they plastered the host team, New Mexico, by 36 points in the semifinals. It was the Lobos' worst loss ever at home. Van Horn then scored 24 to lead Utah past Hawaii in the championship game. It was Utah's first WAC Tournament title.

In 1995, Van Horn led the Utes to the WAC championship.

Utah was rewarded with a fourth seed in the West Regional of the NCAA Tournament. Van Horn struggled in the first round but still scored 21 points as Utah beat Long Beach State, 76–64.

"We just weren't playing our game offensively," Van Horn said. "We were rushing things, and that contributed to our poor shooting. . . . A lot of guys haven't played in the NCAA Tournament before, and everyone was really excited. That threw our shots off."

Utah's shots were thrown off in the second round by Mississippi State center Erick Dampier. In one possession, he blocked two shots by Ben Melmuth and another by Van Horn. Dampier finished the game with 21 points, 10 rebounds, and 8 blocks. MSU beat Utah, 78–64.

"He's strong and very agile," said Van Horn, who had 21 points and 6 rebounds. "When you come down the lane, you know he's going to be there. For all the shots he blocked, he affected just as many."

Majerus said Van Horn learned an important lesson. "Keith is starting to find out [that] heavy is the head that wears the crown," Majerus said. "You want to be the MVP, you have to understand everyone is coming at you."

Still, it was a good season for Van Horn and the Utes. They finished 28–6. They were ranked No. 22 in the country. They won the WAC regular-season championship with a 15–3 record and the WAC Tournament. Van Horn averaged 21 points and 8.5 rebounds a game.

More importantly, Van Horn did not abandon Amy Sida. "There was some tension, but he came over the whole time I was pregnant," Amy said. "He was there when Sabrina was born, and he was there every single day afterward. He was there every single day for Sabrina."

Chapter 6

Father and Player of the Year

Van Horn had a problem on May 30, 1995. He had a paper due for a health-education class, but Amy Sida was in labor.

"I just wrote it in the delivery room," Van Horn said. "Brought in about four books and a few pens and loose-leaf paper. Sabrina was born at about 1:30 A.M. on May 30, and later on I went home and typed up the paper. Had to have it in by 4:00 P.M. . . . . Amy was due, the paper was due. What's so remarkable about what I did?"

The most remarkable part was that in today's society, when athletes often father children and then ignore them, Van Horn stayed put. He changed Sabrina's first diaper. He was there when Sabrina was rushed to the hospital because of dehydration. He was there for the everyday routine of Sabrina's life.

Van Horn worked around his newfound duties to get stronger. Over the summer, he rose from 218 pounds to

242. He became one of the first Utah basketball players ever to bench-press more than three hundred pounds. And he went into the season as a preseason All-American.

Utah started the 1995–96 season against second-ranked Kansas. The Utes were ranked eighth, but they lost, 79–68. Van Horn played well. He scored 22 points, grabbed 10 rebounds, and held KU's star forward, Raef LaFrentz, to 8 points. But it was not good enough for Van Horn.

"It's not a positive because we felt we were just as good a team as them," he said. "It would have only been a positive if they were better than us, which wasn't the case. They just played better."

Utah quickly tried to prove him right. Four days later, the Utes beat fourteenth-ranked Texas on a last-second shot by Ben Caton. A week later, Van Horn had 25 points and 16 rebounds, as Utah drilled Weber State on the road.

Utah's next great test came four days before Christmas. The Utes, ranked No. 13 in the nation, traveled to twelfth-ranked Wake Forest. It was the first head-to-head meeting of Van Horn and fellow All-American junior Tim Duncan. Just nineteen years old, the six-foot ten-inch Duncan came into the game averaging 17 points, 12.5 rebounds, and 5 blocks.

Van Horn had 20 points and 10 rebounds, but Duncan was the difference in Wake's 60–56 win. He had 24 points, 12 rebounds, and 4 blocked shots. He scored ten of the Deacons' last 11 points. And he intimidated Utah into making just three shots in the first eleven and a half minutes.

Some players might have been down after such a big loss, but Van Horn was able to shrug it off. He had something more important to worry about. On Christmas Eve, he asked Amy Sida to marry him. She said yes. They quickly set a wedding date for August, but there was a question about where that wedding might take place.

Right before Christmas of 1995, Van Horn went head-to-head against Tim Duncan of Wake Forest. Both players had good games, but Duncan slightly out-played Van Horn, giving Wake Forest a 60–56 victory.

Van Horn was only a junior and had another season of eligibility at Utah. But he was playing so well that people started asking whether he might enter the NBA draft instead.

"He will, in fact, be a viable candidate [for the draft]," Majerus said. "He's got to decide what he wants. Whatever he wants, I'm 100 percent behind him."

Majerus researched Van Horn's draft potential. One of the people he consulted was Frank Layden, president of the Utah Jazz.

"I don't think he's ready," Layden said. "He's got to learn defensively. I don't know if he can stop anybody. He needs another year of Rick Majerus. But on the other hand, if someone comes and offers him what they're offering . . . how can you tell him not to take that?"

The NBA question hung over Van Horn everywhere he went. In its last home game of the season, Utah held Senior Night to honor the players who were playing their last game in the Huntsman Center.

"Coach and I discussed it," Van Horn joked. "We were thinking about it being Junior Night, too."

Utah won that night, and when it beat Air Force on February 24, it clinched its second straight WAC regular-season championship. The Utes followed that up with an emotional win over BYU. Van Horn scored a career-high 38 points, hit 16 free throws without a miss, and snatched 9 rebounds. He did not miss a shot until only three minutes were left in the game.

He was again named the WAC's Player of the Year, and Utah looked forward to the NCAA Tournament. Utah again received a fourth seed, this time in the Midwest Region.

Utah beat Canisius in the first round, 72–43, without Van Horn. He was in his Dallas hotel room with the flu. In the second round, he got in foul trouble against Iowa State

During the 1995–96 season, the Utes, led by Van Horn, made their first trip to the Sweet Sixteen since 1991. Although Van Horn managed 23 points, Kentucky won 101–70.

and played just 23 minutes. He fouled out with six minutes remaining, but Utah still won, 73–67.

"If someone had told me we were going to the Sweet 16 and Van Horn is only going to play 20 minutes and score 11 points, I would not have thought that possible," Majerus said. "A lot of what we do depends on Van Horn."

It was the Utes' first trip to the Sweet 16 since 1991. But waiting for them was the University of Kentucky, the top-seeded team in the region and one of the favorites for the national championship. The Wildcats played an up-tempo style, pressing the ball full-court on defense and running fast breaks on offense. They also had a deep bench. Many observers felt that their second team would have been ranked in the top 20 by itself.

Kentucky opened a 20-point lead in the first ten minutes of the game. At one point, the Wildcats made 13 straight shots. Van Horn managed 23 points, but Kentucky won, 101–70.

"[Keith] was like a little boy out there," Majerus said. "Keith has to come out of this with a lot of maturation emotionally and physically, whether he tries to go to the next league or stays in our league. Maybe this will be a good thing for him."

"It's impossible to describe how good they are to a person who watched the game," said Van Horn, who finished the season with averages of 21.4 points and 8.8 rebounds.

"This was our worst nightmare," Majerus said.

There was another potential nightmare waiting for Utah fans. Van Horn had to decide whether he was going into the NBA draft or coming back for his senior season.

 Chapter 7

Finishing School

Majerus was not sure Van Horn should turn pro, but Van Horn knew what the money would mean for his family. Amy Sida was working as a waitress. NCAA rules would not allow him to have a job. Sabrina was growing, and there was pressure to support his family.

But Van Horn also wanted his family to stay together. The NBA lifestyle would keep him away from home a lot; the season ran from early October to late April, even longer if his team made the playoffs. He also had promised his father that he would get his degree.

Van Horn discussed his choice with Frank Layden and his son Scott Layden, who was the general manager for the Jazz. He discussed it with former Utah football star Jamal Anderson, who was a star running back for the Atlanta Falcons. He talked to teammates Michael Doleac and Andre Miller about the team's chances if he stayed. Finally, he talked to Majerus over a three-hour lunch.

Finally, on April 11, 1996, Van Horn announced he was staying at Utah.

"I've seen through Amy and Sabrina that basketball

isn't the most important thing in my life," Van Horn said. "Having a baby put my life in focus. It's always bothered me when fathers don't play a role in their child's life, not just financially but in other ways."

"Keith showed a lot of character and wisdom by staying in school," said Scott Layden. "He's lucky. He's surrounded by people who care about him and gave him good guidance. He should be thankful for that."

Van Horn was even more thankful when he married Amy Sida in August.

"We had our ups and downs," she said, "but it never occurred to me that Keith would just leave. I knew that whatever happened would happen for the best. Now, while we're still here in Utah, we've had a year to get together, build a family and really got to know each other."

Utah was the easy preseason pick to win the WAC again, even though the league had expanded from ten to sixteen teams. Van Horn was named a preseason All-American by every publication possible, and Utah was rated No. 5 in the country by CNN/USA Today.

But Van Horn quickly went into a slump. In early December, he was averaging a career-low 16 points. His shooting percentage was 34 percent.

Majerus finally pulled him aside and said, "You know you're a pretty good player, right?"

Van Horn shrugged. "Well, let me remind you, then," Majerus said. "Keep doing what you're doing because you're the best there is at doing it."

In Utah's next game, Van Horn took Majerus at his word and scored 41 points against Weber State. A week later, he blitzed fourteenth-ranked Texas with 34 points and 12 rebounds. Then he scored his 2,000th career point against Wisconsin–Milwaukee. Only two other Utes—Billy McGill (2,331) and Josh Grant (2,000)—ever scored that many.

At the end of his junior year, Van Horn had to make one of the toughest decisions of his life. Should he stay at Utah for his senior year, or enter the NBA draft?

On New Year's Eve, second-ranked Wake Forest came to Utah. As happened the previous year, Tim Duncan dominated the game. He had 23 points, 16 rebounds, 8 assists, and 3 blocks. Van Horn played well, too, scoring Utah's first 9 points and finishing with 24. But he was recovering from the flu and got tired in the second half. Wake Forest pulled away for a 70–59 win.

Still, Van Horn was playing well. In the five weeks after his pep talk from Majerus, Van Horn averaged 26.2 points, 10.7 rebounds, and shot 55 percent.

He did not stop there. He scored 33 in a win at Colorado State. He lit up Texas Christian for 40. Then he broke McGill's Utah career scoring record in a win at Tulsa.

"When I look back at my college career, it's not one of the things I'll remember the most," Van Horn said about the record. "I'll remember the conference championships and the good times I've had with my teammates . . . I've never been one to really focus on individual stats and records."

More important to Van Horn was Senior Night at Utah's last home game of the season. He hit his first five shots, including four three-pointers, on his way to 29 points and 6 rebounds. Utah beat eleventh-ranked New Mexico, 78–58, to run its record to 23–3 overall and 15–1 in the WAC.

After the game, Van Horn told the crowd, "This is the best way to go out. This has been the greatest four years of my life."

"Our fans grew with Keith, and that night was like kissing him good-bye," said Utah athletic director Chris Hill. "There was a warmth there for Keith and for the team that everyone could feel."

The Utes carried that warmth into the WAC Tournament. Van Horn's last-second heroics in the tournament's early games and a drilling of Texas Christian in the championship game sent them into the 1997 NCAA Tournament with momentum.

The NCAA Tournament started with a 75–61 win over Navy. Van Horn had 16 points and 11 rebounds; he also broke Danny Ainge's all-time WAC scoring record. Then he scored 27 against North Carolina–Charlotte in the second round, and Utah won, 77–58. That set up a Sweet 16 game against Stanford.

Stanford was not a traditional basketball powerhouse. However, it beat Wake Forest in the tourney's second round by banging Duncan with six players who were at least six feet seven inches and 225 pounds. Duncan, the National Player of the Year, had just 4 points and 5 rebounds in his last college game.

"They're a very physical and strong team, and we have to play through that," Majerus said. "They defense like an NBA team. They put the forearm in your back and push out."

Utah played great defense in the first half. Stanford's All-American point guard, Brevin Knight, scored just 2 points. But he came alive in the second half with 25, including an 8-point flurry in the last thirty-nine seconds to tie the game.

Van Horn struggled with his shot, making just 9 of 26, but he managed to score 25 points and grab 14 rebounds. But thirty-four seconds into overtime, he fouled out. Utah seemed doomed to fall in the Sweet 16 again.

Van Horn gathered the Utes for a quick huddle. He told them he believed in them. He said they had won without him before. He said they could do it again.

Majerus shifted the focus of the offense to Doleac and freshman Hanna Mottola, who drew foul after foul from Stanford. Andre Miller also scored five points in overtime. Utah survived, 82–77.

"This was a great game," Majerus said. "I don't know if there's a better game in the tournament."

But it did set up a better matchup—Utah against Kentucky again, this time for the chance to go to the Final Four.

Kentucky led 34–20 at halftime, but Utah tied the game with 9:32 to go. Kentucky responded with a 9–2 run, then

At the end of a difficult 1996–97 season, the Utes took the WAC championship. Unfortunately, they were unable to reach the Final Four of the NCAA tournament.

Utah lost Miller when he reinjured a sore wrist with 4:42 remaining.

Kentucky won 72–59. Van Horn's college career was over.

"I really don't know what my emotions are," he said after the game. "It's tough to know that I'm not going to play with these guys anymore . . . I just want to remember all the good things that have happened. Obviously, I'm disappointed in the loss right now, but we have had a good season."

He had also had a good college career. In Van Horn's four years, the Utes were 98–31. They had gone 84–17 since his disastrous freshman season. They had also become one of the top 10 college teams of the 1990s with a winning percentage of .741. He was a consensus All-American. He even won an ESPY from ESPN as Male College Basketball Player of the Year.

More importantly, he had survived—and thrived—under Rick Majerus.

"He's been like a father figure to me," Van Horn said. "I grew up a lot in my four years there. I experienced a lot, and he was with me through the good times and the bad. We'll always have a special relationship."

Chapter 8

Immediate Impact

John Calipari wanted to change "the culture of losing" of the New Jersey Nets. He saw Van Horn as a key to doing that.

But Van Horn was sure to go in the first three picks of the 1997 NBA Draft, and New Jersey had the seventh slot. So Calipari arranged a trade. Philadelphia drafted Van Horn with the second pick, then sent him to New Jersey in a seven-player deal.

"This was another big step for us," Calipari said. "In all the workouts we had, he stood out head and shoulders above everybody else. . . . We're not looking at Keith Van Horn as our savior. We're looking at him . . . as a player who adds great versatility."

That versatility led to comparisons with Boston Celtics legend Larry Bird, which Van Horn did his best to stop. "I think people will realize that I'm a different player," he said. "I think people may compare us . . . just because we're both six feet nine inches and white. But once they see us as players, there will be some differences."

There were a lot of differences in Van Horn's personal

life, too. He moved from the quiet, slow pace of Utah to the fast-paced East Coast. Amy had their second baby, a son named Nicholas, three weeks before the draft. When he signed his contract in late July, Van Horn was a millionaire.

He averaged 14 points and 4 rebounds in seven preseason games. But he injured his ankle a week before the

Head Coach John Calipari wanted the New Jersey Nets to be winners. He decided early on that acquiring Van Horn was key to building a strong team.

regular season started. He missed the first 17 games of the season, including the Nets' only trip to Utah.

He finally made his NBA debut December 5th against Philadelphia. He scored 11 points in 26 minutes, and New Jersey won easily, 107–88.

Off the court, Van Horn and teammate Jayson Williams became fast friends. They had worked out together during the summer, and their differing personalities were like magnets for each other. Williams was probably the most outgoing man in the league; Van Horn was quiet. Williams was the veteran showing the rookie the ropes; Van Horn was the energetic rookie giving new life to a player used to the "culture of losing."

Things were going well for Van Horn, but the endless comparisons to Bird were annoying—especially when Detroit's Brian Williams said Van Horn got star treatment from the referees because he was "The Great White Hope."

"I would like to prove myself on the court before people start declaring I'm a future star," Van Horn said. "I haven't proven anything yet. Hopefully, they'll be talking about me because I'm a player, not because I'm a white player, by the end of the season."

In late January, the people in Utah were talking about him as a great player. The Utes retired his uniform number, forty-four. Van Horn told the crowd, "You people here will never know how much you meant to me. I've never said that publicly before, but the support I got from the fans after my father died is the most important thing I've ever been given."

A week later, Van Horn was showered with attention again—this time at All-Star Weekend in New York City. He played in the Rookies Game and had 17 points and 10 rebounds in 25 minutes.

"This is crazy," Van Horn said about the media attention. "I've never seen anything like this before. It's probably the wildest event I've ever attended. It just seems like a big circus to me."

After the All-Star break, Van Horn scored 24 in a win over Toronto and a career-high 35 in a victory against Detroit. By February 17, the Nets were 31–22. They were just four games behind Miami for first place in the Atlantic Division.

But then Van Horn "hit the wall," which means that the grind of the NBA schedule wore him out. In one five-game stretch he shot just 29 percent.

"I'm more tired than I was a month ago," Van Horn said. "It's just a few bad games, that's all. Sometimes you play so many games you don't really realize what you're doing wrong."

Things got worse March 2nd when Van Horn broke the index toe on his right foot against Utah. He reinjured the toe against Charlotte, then finally pulled himself out of a game in San Antonio because of the pain.

The Nets were slumping, too. A few weeks after talking about winning their division, they were battling just to make the playoffs. Back in Utah, things were going well for the Utes, who finally made it to the Final Four.

"I felt like I had to get off the phone [when Van Horn called]," Michael Doleac said. "It was a little depressing. He was so happy for us, but I got the feeling he wishes he was going with us."

"I just wish I could have gotten him here," Majerus said.

Van Horn did not even go to the Final Four to cheer for Utah; he stayed in New Jersey to concentrate on making the playoffs. Utah won the semifinal game against North Carolina but then lost to Kentucky again, this time for the national championship.

Keith Van Horn tries to fly by Alonzo Mourning. Van Horn had to use all the skills he learned from Majerus to make it in the NBA.

Meanwhile, the Nets lost to Washington to drop out of the final playoff spot, then moved back into that slot with a win over the 76ers. Van Horn scored 31 in that win and won a pivotal jump ball with twenty-two seconds left to play, but he also reinjured his toe.

Williams broke his thumb against Boston two nights later, but the Nets refused to fold. They won big games against the Knicks and the Hawks. And when they beat Toronto on April 12th, the Nets needed just one win to clinch their first playoff spot since 1994.

During that game, Van Horn suffered another injury. He fell on his right wrist, which was his shooting arm. He told Calipari not to run any plays for him to shoot outside. He then scored a career-high 33 close to the basket.

New Jersey finally clinched a playoff spot eight days later with a 114–101 win over Detroit. Van Horn scored 25, including 16 in the first half.

"Making the playoffs was the only goal I set for myself this year," he said after the game.

That was a good thing, because the Nets were not going any further. Their first-round opponents were Michael Jordan's Chicago Bulls, winners of five NBA titles in the 1990s.

"This is a great way to go," Calipari said before the series started. "If you're going to learn what the playoffs are really about, why not do it against the team that's won . . . five [championships]? Now you're going to learn exactly what it is we need to do."

In the first game in Chicago, Van Horn missed most of the game because he had a strep infection. Point guard Sam Cassell—the only Net with significant playoff experience—reinjured a sore groin muscle in the third period. New Jersey still forced the Bulls into overtime before losing, 96–93.

Van Horn felt better for the second game in the

best-of-five series, but he got in early foul trouble. He had only 10 points and 5 rebounds in 28 minutes, and the Bulls won again. Then Chicago ended the Nets' season with a 116–101 win in New Jersey.

"This is our first step," Calipari said. "I want to build from it. We have a chance to be really good. We have a lot of young players with talent."

Van Horn was the leader of that group. He averaged 19.7 points and 6.6 rebounds per game. He finished second to Duncan in voting for Rookie of the Year. And he led New Jersey to a 43–39 record, its best in four years.

"I've been through a lot this year," Van Horn said. "This team went through a lot. . . . Sometimes, when you end a season, you don't look forward to the next season, but I'm looking forward to it."

He would have to wait longer than he ever dreamed for it to arrive.

Chapter 9

Disappointing Seasons

The NBA locked out its players July 1, 1998. The NBA management disagreed with the players about how much money they should make. The league locked its doors and said there would be no basketball until a new deal was reached. The lockout lingered for months, and by September, Van Horn was frustrated.

"The biggest thing the fans need to realize is the owners are doing this," he said. "If they're going to be mad at anyone, be mad at the owners because they initiated the lockout. This is an owners' strike."

But by early January, both sides were arguing about numbers so large that normal fans thought they were crazy. Van Horn joined Jayson Williams and Toronto's Kevin Willis in asking that the players vote on the owners' latest proposal.

In mid-January—with the season about to be canceled—the two sides made a deal. There would be a shortened season of 50 games starting in February. Many players—including Van Horn—were glad the lockout was over.

"To tell you the truth," Van Horn said, "I'd rather lose $30 million [in my contract] than be a guy making so much that there was no one else around on the team. I'd rather take less—much less—and win a championship than break the bank and be on a team that went nowhere."

Unfortunately, he really was on a team that went nowhere. The Nets lost Cassell to a sprained ankle in their first game and finished February with a 2–10 record. Cassell was injured off and on for the entire month, and fellow starters Kerry Kittles and Rony Seikaly missed games, too.

The Nets won their third game March 1st, when Van Horn hit a shot at the buzzer against Boston. But then they lost to Charlotte despite 28 points and 9 rebounds by Van Horn. Worried that losing would tear the team apart, Van Horn met with the coaches after the game.

"I just wanted to make sure that we are trying to keep this team together, keep everyone's head together, keep people from going off on their own ways," he said. "There's nothing worse than losing and having a bunch of guys not liking each other. . . . I understand the clock is ticking, but if we stick through this, maybe we can salvage the season."

Desperate for a change, the Nets traded for Minnesota point guard Stephon Marbury in early March. Among those traded from New Jersey was Cassell, who played in just four of the team's first 16 games.

A few days later, a Nets loss in Miami dropped them to 3–17. After that game, Nets owner Lewis Katz marched Calipari to his limousine and fired him.

"That organization is fragile," Cassell said. "The blame was going on me and then [Calipari], which is not fair. When I went down, guys didn't step up. Keith Van Horn was doing his part, but there were other guys that weren't stepping up."

Assistant Coach Don Casey became the new head coach, but the team continued to struggle with injuries. Van Horn missed a pair of games because of a sprained ankle. Center Jim McIlvaine tore cartilage in his shoulder. Jayson Williams shattered his leg. Finally, with less than a week left in the season, Van Horn broke his thumb.

The lost season did not hurt Van Horn's bargaining position. He had only one year left on his contract.

The New Jersey Nets were in shambles during Van Horn's second season. Calipari was fired, and players were traded. It was up to the injured Van Horn to keep the team together.

Worried that Van Horn might want to sign with Utah, New Jersey signed him to a six-year contract extension worth $73 million.

Trying to forget the 1999 disaster, Van Horn hit the weight room again. He rose to 250 pounds and dropped his body fat to 5.9 percent. He also worked on finishing shots around the basket.

A lot was expected from the Nets. They were the only team with two returning players among the league's top 10 scorers of the previous season—Van Horn was fifth (21.8), and Marbury was eighth (21.3).

But there were warning signs that the Nets might struggle. Marbury took too many shots. Williams still had not recovered from his broken leg. And shooting guard Kenny Kittles was recovering slowly from knee surgery.

Van Horn shot miserably in the first few weeks of the season, and Marbury tried to win games by himself. The Nets began the season at 2–15, their worst start ever.

"Our big players aren't making big plays," Casey said after a loss at Sacramento. "What else can I say? I can't hide it any longer. I think [Keith's] pressing."

Finally, Majerus had seen enough. He sent a letter to Van Horn, then called him to offer advice.

"(He) was trying to remind me of the player that I was," Van Horn said. "All the intensity, all the energy that I brought to the game. He wanted me to remember that I had it in me. . . . He really felt that I was putting too much pressure on myself. He said to try and get some easy buckets, and once you do that the rim will open up for you."

Van Horn got another boost, too. After playing just seven minutes in the first 14 games of the season, Kittles returned to the starting lineup. The Nets started winning. They beat Sacramento behind 21 second-half points from Van Horn. He scored 20 in a win over Milwaukee. He scored 21 in a win over Houston. He made 33 of 51 shots over a four-game stretch, and the Nets were 10–3 in December.

The Nets went into the All-Star break, 19–30. They were 17–15 since the horrific 2–15 start. They could still make the playoffs, but they needed to play well in the second half of the season to do it.

They got off to another bad start in the second half. The Nets' first game after the break was in Atlanta, but the night before the game, Amy went into labor. She had their third child, a girl named Noelle, the next day. Van Horn missed that night's game, and Atlanta won, 103–86.

"It's not an issue," he said about missing the game. "I thought it was best for my family. I think we all understand that your family should take precedence over your career."

With his game in another funk in late February, Van Horn watched videotape with Assistant Coach Jim Lynam. They decided Van Horn had to be more aggressive on offense. He had to drive to the basket. He needed to finish more shots.

In his next game, Van Horn did just that against Charlotte. He made 12 of 16 shots, grabbed 11 rebounds, and scored 29 points. New Jersey won by 11.

Two nights later, Van Horn scored 18 points and had 13 rebounds in his first professional game in Utah. He got a standing ovation from the crowd when he was introduced before the game, but he was booed in the fourth quarter when the score was close.

"Hey, they're still Jazz fans, and 30 percent of those people in the stands went to BYU anyway, so I could understand it," said Van Horn, whose Nets lost to the Jazz, 106–101.

Van Horn kept playing well. He scored 25 in a win at Denver. He hit a last-second shot to beat Dallas. The Nets improved to 26–36, just three and a half games out of the

During a turning point in the Nets 1998–99 season, Assistant Coach Jim Lyman decided that Van Horn needed to be more aggressive. Van Horn took his advice and scored 29 points in the next game.

final playoff spot in the Eastern Conference. And they expected a boost because Williams was finally ready to play.

But in his first practice, Williams went up for a rebound, landed on a teammate's shoe, and broke his foot. His season was over, and he would soon retire.

"He was playing unbelievably—rebounding, dunking, knocking down some jumpers," Van Horn said. "We kind of expected that boost, and now we're not going to get it. We just have to depend on the guys we have been depending on."

But those guys were falling apart, too. Marbury developed tendinitis in his knee. Kittles' knee started to hurt again. By early April, the Nets had just nine healthy players, and one of those was a Continental Basketball Association (CBA) player on a ten-day contract. They lost their last 11 games.

"Before all these injuries happened to us the past couple of weeks," Van Horn said, "we were playing like a playoff-caliber basketball team. It was unfortunate. We're missing three starters, three key players. There's no way around it. It's tough to win when you're missing like that."

The Nets finished 31–51, their twelfth 50-loss season in their twenty-four years in the NBA. They were 2–26 in the losing streaks that started and ended the season, 29–25 in between.

Casey was fired a week after the season. Team president Michael Rowe resigned to avoid being fired, himself.

And over the summer, Van Horn worked harder than ever, trying to turn the Nets into winners.

Chapter 10

Ready to Improve

Van Horn had finished three seasons in the NBA. Despite the Nets' problems, his career statistics were impressive—19.9 points and 7.8 rebounds per game. And he would get better with experience.

"The more Van Horn can give them, the better [the Nets] become," said Basketball Hall of Famer Jack Ramsey, a former NBA head coach and current ESPN analyst. "If Van Horn can give the Nets 20 points and 10 rebounds a night, the Nets would be vastly improved. I spent some time with him during the [1999–00] preseason, and I got to work on his offensive game. He should be virtually unstoppable, like a Kevin Garnett-type of player."

"What third-year player is a finished product?" Van Horn asked. "I don't think I've necessarily played the way I'm capable of. But it's not like I'm sitting here averaging 13 points and five or six rebounds per game. I'm literally this close to being where I was and even better than where I was. I just need an extra push to get to that next level."

"Keith is going to take a couple of more years before he reaches his potential," said New Jersey teammate Kendall

Gill, a ten-year NBA veteran. "He's gone around the league a few times, and players have adjusted to his game. Now he needs to adjust to them. When he does that, he's going to be just fine."

"His third year, Garnett was averaging 17 points and eight or nine rebounds per game," Van Horn said. "Now he's at 23 (points) and 12 (rebounds) five years into the

Wearing the striped hat, Keith Van Horn sits beside NBA commissioner David Stern. The NBA reading program is only one of the many charities Van Horn participates in.

league. There's an opportunity for a tremendous amount of improvement between your third and seventh years in the league."

Off the court, Van Horn was already an all-star. He was devoted to his family. He was committed to his charity work with the Special Olympics, Catholic Community Charities, and the NBA's Reading program. He still worked toward his degree, now with a major in sociology. And he remained committed to living in New Jersey.

"If I were to retire today, I would definitely live on the East Coast," he said. "I love to go back (to California); I love to see the beach and I love the ocean. But the smog and the earthquakes and mudslides and traffic, it just wears on you. . . . I like the big city. I like the fact I can be in New York in a half-hour. I can be at the beach in 45 minutes. Six hours from Europe, three hours from Miami. I feel like I'm close to everything."

But the most important thing he is close to is people—his teammates, his friends, and his family.

"If my son grows up to be the man that Keith is, I'm going to kiss my wife so hard on the lips she won't know what hit her," Calipari said.

Majerus, who's been Van Horn's toughest critic in many ways, echoed that thought: "He's a wonderful human being."

Career Statistics
College

Season	GP	FGM	FGA	FG%	REB	AST	PTS	PPG
1993–94	25	161	312	.516	208	21	457	18.3
1994–95	33	246	451	.545	280	45	694	21.0
1995–96	32	236	439	.538	283	31	686	21.4
1996–97	32	248	504	.492	303	45	705	22.0
Totals	122	891	1,706	.522	1,074	142	2,542	20.8

NBA

Season	GP	FGM	FGA	FG%	REB	AST	STL	BLK	PTS	RPG	PPG
1997–98	62	446	1,047	.426	408	106	64	25	1,219	6.6	19.7
1998–99	42	322	752	.428	358	65	43	53	916	8.5	21.8
1999–00	80	559	1,257	.445	676	158	64	60	1,535	8.5	19.2
2000–01	49	308	708	.435	347	82	40	20	831	7.1	17.0
Totals	233	1,635	3,764	.432	1,789	411	211	158	4,501	7.8	19.3

GP=Games Played FG%=Field Goal Percentage FGA=Field Goal Attempts
FGM=Field Goals Made REB=Rebounds AST=Assists
STL=Steals BLK=Blocks PTS=Points
PPG=Points Per Game RPG=Rebounds Per Game

Where to Write Keith Van Horn

Keith Van Horn
c/o New Jersey Nets
390 Murray Hill Parkway
East Rutherford, NJ 07073

On the Internet at:

http://www.nba.com/playerfile/keith_van_horn.html
http://sports.espn.go.com/nba/players/profile?statsid=3169

Index